Welcome to the CRANIUM Word Worm Book of Outrageous Fun!

If you've ever told a story, done a word puzzle, or made up a poem, you've wandered into the witty and wonderful world of Word Worm. You don't have to be a bookworm to have a blast—it's all about having fun with your imagination. With Word Worm by your side, you'll spin stories, unpuzzle puzzles, and have outrageous fun along the way!

What's Inside...

Word Worm's activity pages are overflowing with things to do! Go through the pages in any order and make your mark with the purple pen when inspiration strikes. Be on the lookout for special rewritable pages marked with **RW**, where you can use the eraser to start over whenever you want, making your creations different and more outrageous each time. Want to double the fun? You can play together with a friend at the places marked

Word Worm's pals **Creative Cat**, **Data Head**, and **Star Performer** are along for the ride, introducing all kinds of activities, puzzles, and fun facts along the way.

 Creative Cat will get you sketching and stretching your imagination—even sculpting with his purple clay!

 Data Head will zip in to share fun facts about all kinds of topics and get you solving your way through one-of-a-kind puzzles and mazes.

And when **Star Performer** is on the scene, get ready to jump out of your seat for playful fun!

Super Sign-In Pages

Near the back of the book you'll find *Word Worm's Super Sign-In Pages*, with outrageous questions you never thought to ask yourself or your friends and family. Pass your book around and get everyone to sign in—you won't believe the funny things you'll learn about the people you thought you knew best!

Cool Cranium Stuff...and Mini Letter Line-Up Game!

Open the clear plastic drawer to find Word Worm's Letter Cubes and all the other things you'll use for the activity pages and Word Worm's Mini Letter Line-Up Game: a cool erasable marker and special purple eraser, a tub of purple Cranium Clay, a mini timer, 25 game cards, a die, and a mover piece. Now slide the entire drawer out to the right to reveal the hidden game board, where you can play Mini Letter Line-Up with your friends. Mix and match your **Cranium Books of Outrageous Fun!** to create your own new Cranium games—or collect all four to complete your set!

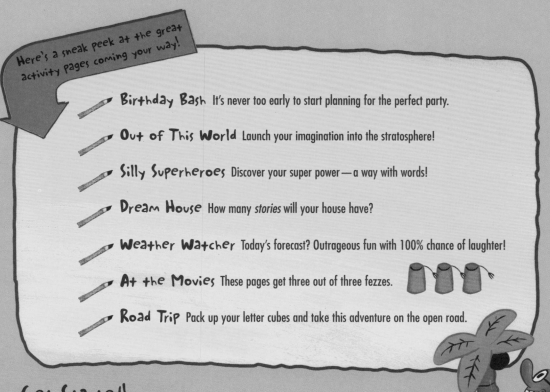

Here's a sneak peek at the great activity pages coming your way!

Birthday Bash It's never too early to start planning for the perfect party.

Out of This World Launch your imagination into the stratosphere!

Silly Superheroes Discover your super power—a way with words!

Dream House How many *stories* will your house have?

Weather Watcher Today's forecast? Outrageous fun with 100% chance of laughter!

At the Movies These pages get three out of three fezzes.

Road Trip Pack up your letter cubes and take this adventure on the open road.

Get Started!

It's time to kick off Word Worm's wacky wordplay. Let the outrageous fun begin!

birthday BASH

An inviting invitation is just the ticket!

It doesn't matter if your birthday is minutes or months away—it's never too soon to start planning your party, especially if it's going to be the best of the best!

LOOK!

THE RIGHT INVITE

Are you ready to write an invitation worthy of the world's best birthday party? Don't worry—it's as easy as blowing out a birthday candle. All you need to do is answer the questions below by writing directly into your invitation.

1. How old you'll be on your next birthday
2. Something you'd love to travel in
3. Something you'd like to have in your backyard
4. Someone you don't get to see very often
5. A celebrity you love
6. The number of presents you got for your last birthday
7. Your favorite ice-cream flavor
8. Your favorite candy
9. A fun thing to draw
10. A food you love to eat for dinner
11. Your most comfortable piece of furniture
12. Your favorite city in the world
13. Your favorite game to play indoors
14. Your favorite game or sport to play outside
15. A fun thing to do on weekends
16. Your favorite singer
17. A birthday present you would love to get
18. Something you enjoy sharing with your friends

Sculpt it! Roll the Cranium Clay into long tubular shapes, then use them to write your name in fancy letters on top of your birthday cake. Use the remaining clay to sculpt tiny decorations for your cake.

YOU'RE A V.I.P.
(Very Important Person)
INVITED TO A V.I.B.P.!
(Very Important Birthday Party)

In honor of _____'s _____ trips around the Sun, please come to the world's
           your name   1

best birthday celebration! I have a fantastic day planned. Here's the schedule:

First thing in the morning, a(n) _____ will pick you up and bring you to my house, where we've
                             2

built a(n) _____ just for this party. A few special friends, _____ and
           3   4

_____, will be joining us for the celebration. And don't forget to bring your appetite! We'll
  5

have a special cake made of _____ layers of _____ cake with _____ in
                     6   7   8

between. The cake will be designed by a famous artist in the shape of a(n) _____. Of course
                                                   9

we'll have other food too: all the _____ you can eat. Afterwards, we'll travel by jet-powered
                          10

_____ to downtown _____, where we will play as much
           11   12

_____ and _____ as we want. Or you can just
           13   14

_____ all afternoon!
           15

I almost forgot — before we leave, _____ will lead us all in a special version of "Happy Birthday"!
                                16

One more thing: Of course you don't have to get me a present. But if you insist, here are a couple of ideas:

_____ or _____ to share with everyone.
           17   18

I can't wait to see you!

Your festive friend,

_____
your signature

age: _____ years _____ months

Draw it!

Decorate the border of your invitation with drawings of
balloons and other things you want to have at your party —
or funny pictures of you and your guests during the party.

RW

5

Draw your own silly card!

FUN FACT

Blowing out candles on a cake is a birthday tradition celebrated throughout the world, but did you know that some countries have other special birthday traditions? In Argentina, a child receives a pull on the earlobe for each year old, and in Denmark kids hang a flag outside their windows to let people passing by know that they are enjoying a birthday celebration inside.

If you could invent a new birthday tradition, what would it be?
What would you like everyone to do on YOUR birthday?
Write it here:

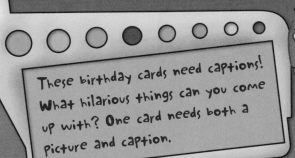

These birthday cards need captions! What hilarious things can you come up with? One card needs both a picture and caption.

Write it!

Next time you sing "Happy Birthday," use our Song-O-Matic to come up with some silly new endings. Just choose one phrase from each column, put them together, and sing them as the last two lines of the song. Try different combinations—or write your own!

"Happy birthday to you, happy birthday to you…"

SONG-O-MATIC

You walk like a duck,	and you talk like one too.
You dance like a penguin,	and you sing like one too.
You smile like a walrus,	and you belong in a zoo.
You laugh like a hyena,	and you smell like one too.
You snort like a pig,	but I still do love you.
You _____ like a _____,	and you _____ like one too.

What would you like for your next birthday? Here's one way to generate a list: Roll the letter cubes and write down all the things you want that start with the letters you rolled.

PRESENT GENERATOR

1 _____   2 _____   3 _____   4 _____

_____

_____

_____

_____

OUT OF THIS WORLD

Think you need a rocket ship and a fancy spacesuit to explore outer space? Think again! You can have incredible adventures in far-off places with just these pages and your imagination.

I love having all this SPACE to express myself.

Congratulations! You made it through astronaut-training school and have been chosen to be on the next trip into outer space. Use your answers from this list to fill in the story and learn more about your exciting mission:

1. A planet other than Earth

2. A word describing a test you had to take

3. The number of people in your school

4. A word describing an alien

5. The color of your eyes

6. Something you rode in or on during the last month

7. The number of teeth you have

8. Animals at the zoo

9. The first digit of your phone number

10. Your favorite thing to read about

11. The name of one of your neighbors' pets

12. A word describing the last food you ate

13. The time left until your next birthday

14. Someone you think is really funny

15. Something you're really looking forward to

16. Something in your room

17. Your favorite item of clothing

18. A creepy insect

INTERGALACTIC COUNCIL

OFFICIAL DOCUMENTS

Write it!

Greetings!

As you know, you've been picked to travel to _____. The selection
                                                              1

process was very _____, and you were the only one out of
                              2

_____ people chosen to make this _____ journey.
            3   **4**

Now that you've joined the team, prepare to travel in style. The _____
                                                                              5

space _____ has _____ engines,
                  6   **7**

which have been tuned up by specially trained _____.
                                                              8

Inside the vehicle, there is enough room for _____
                                                          9

_____-lovers, plus a special compartment for _____.
          10   **11**

As for the food, all of it is super _____ once you get used to it.
                                              12

The trip will take about _____, unless of course you run into
                                    13

_____ — and then it's anyone's guess as to how long you'll be delayed.
          14

Don't worry, though, we'll have you back in time for _____. Oh, and
                                                                  15

one last thing: You don't need to worry about packing a(n) _____,
                                                                        16

because we will give you a new _____ to last the entire trip.
                                            17

Have a safe journey, and be sure to watch out for space _____s!
                                                                      18

Moon Log: A Nighttime Activity

The key to becoming a good scientist is being a good observer. Start practicing your scientific-observer skills by taking a look at the Moon—it's an illuminating thing to study because it looks different every day.

Your location: _____

Today's date: _____   Time: _____

Brief weather report (clear? cloudy?): _____

Tonight the Moon is missing/small/half/big/full.
                        (circle one)

Other observations (for example, is the Moon up high in the sky or low? Do you see any

stars nearby?): _____

_____

Predictions:

I think tomorrow night the Moon will look bigger/smaller.
                                        (circle one)

I think the Moon will be full in _____ days.

CHECK BACK TOMORROW OR IN A COUPLE OF DAYS TO SEE IF YOUR PREDICTIONS WERE RIGHT.

Draw it!

The different shapes of the Moon are perfect for artistic inspiration! Draw the shape of tonight's Moon, then add your own twist to turn your sketch into an artistic masterpiece. Many people see a face in the patterns on the Moon. Draw your own "man (or woman) in the moon." Do you see a cow jumping over the moon? Draw your own moonscape in the space below.

FIND A FRIEND!

TAKE TURNS DRAWING A MOONSCAPE. CAN YOUR FRIEND GUESS WHAT YOU SEE IN YOUR MOON? NOW SWITCH!

Solve it!

Test your cosmic knowledge with this Planetary Pop Quiz. Circle the correct answer.

1. Saturn is the only planet that has rings around it.   True/False

2. The Sun is a star.   True/False

3. The Moon is older than the Earth.   True/False

? Turn to page 36 to check your answers.

Solve it!

Here's a silly saying for remembering the planets in the order of their distance from the Sun. Each planet begins with the first letter of each word in this phrase: My Very Eager Mother Just Served Us Nine Pizzas. Unscramble the letters next to each of these words to identify the planet.

My:	ERCMUYR
Very:	USVNE
Eager:	AETHR
Mother:	MRSA
Just:	RIUPTJE

Served:	TSAUNR
Us:	SURNUA
Nine:	PTENEUN
Pizzas:	OPTUL

? Turn to page 36 to check your answers.

FUN FACT

Photo: Michael K. Fairbanks, DPM

Did you know that our nightly neighbor, the Moon, has a lot to do with how we measure time into months? Even its name can be traced back to Greek and Latin words for "month" and "to measure." There is a full moon every 29 days, 12 hours, and 44 minutes. How many moons until your birthday?

SILLY SUPERHEROES

Ready to do some silly writing? Find out what happens when you combine your ideas about "silly" and "superhero"!

Words to the rescue!

Write it!

Here's a story that needs some help. Check out the list below, then fill in the story with your answers. Try it a few different ways—new answers will give you a whole new superhero scenario!

1. How you feel when first waking up

2. A vegetable you have to eat way too often

3. An animal you'd like to be

4. A really sweet dessert

5. Something you like to put in a sandwich

6. Something you're always losing

7. Something really smelly

8. A smell you love

FUN FACT

Sometimes real people accomplish superpowered (but silly) physical challenges. In 1991, a team of 14 college students covered 996 miles (1,603 km) in 10 days—by leapfrogging!

The Adventures of _____ Woman
1

_____ Woman isn't your average superhero. She gets her super powers
1

from eating _____ and travels on the back of an ill-tempered
2

_____. When people see her in her superhero outfit, they can't help
3

but smile. She usually wears _____-colored tights and a cape made
4

out of dried _____.
5

_____ Woman's mission is to help people who can't find their
1

_____, but her sense of direction isn't so hot—she's always
6

getting herself lost. On one mission, she was trying to help someone search for

_____, when she got lost in the back of a truck filled with
6

_____. Luckily, a fellow superhero named Captain
7

_____, whose mission is to eliminate bad odors, was soon on the
8

scene. She was back in business. She found the lost item, reunited it with its owner, and rescued a

kitten from a tree on her way home just for fun. Of course, she got lost on the way home, but that's

another story....

Draw it! Use this space to draw scenes from your story.

RW

SILLY SUPERHERO-O-MATIC

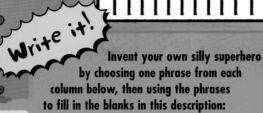

Write it!

Invent your own silly superhero by choosing one phrase from each column below, then using the phrases to fill in the blanks in this description:

INSERT COIN HERE

ONLY!! 5¢

It's Amazing Captain _____
word from column A

who can _____—and
phrase from column B

always _____!
phrase from column C

WARNING: DO NOT PUSH

Column A

Tofu

Birdbrain

Muscleman

Mosquito

_____

_____

_____

three nouns that begin with a letter on your letter cubes

Column B

see through walls

give a good haircut

cross his eyes

rescue burned meals

_____

_____

_____

three super powers

Column C

chews on garlic

says the wrong thing

arrives everywhere late

speaks in rhyme

_____

_____

_____

three silly actions

Come up with your own ideas for each column!

FIND A FRIEND!

TAKE TURNS COMING UP WITH SILLY SUPERHEROES USING THE SILLY SUPERHERO-O-MATIC. ACT LIKE YOUR HERO AND SEE IF YOUR FRIEND CAN GUESS WHAT YOUR SILLY SUPER POWERS ARE.

Draw it!

A-Mazing Superhero

Can you use your maze-solving super powers to get
from START to FINISH by collecting exactly 50 points?

START

FINISH

Turn to page 36 to check your answers.

DREAM HOUSE

I love doing house-work!

Welcome home! This isn't just any ordinary place to live — you already have one of those. You'll be creating a house so perfect that only **YOU** could have come up with the idea.

Write it!

Building a real house takes a lot of time and work, but building a dream house is as easy as imagining your favorite things all together in one place. Now you can build your perfect place in 12 easy steps. Just check out the items below, add your answers into the story, and you're on your way to a heavenly house!

1. A relative who lives far away
2. Something you shout when you're really excited
3. The number of years you've been in school
4. Your favorite city
5. Something you have that no one else you know has
6. A scary-looking animal
7. A name that starts with a letter you roll with one of your letter cubes
8. A type of tree that grows near where you live
9. A flower that smells great
10. The number of books in your room
11. The age of the oldest person in your family
12. A game or sport you like to play over the weekend

FUN FACT

When dreaming of a house, it's almost impossible to think too big. Take the 17th-century home of King Louis XIV, for example. Located just outside of Paris, France, the Palace of Versailles is famous for its enormous Hall of Mirrors. This huge hall, lined with 17 oversized mirrors, is as long as a 24-story building is tall!

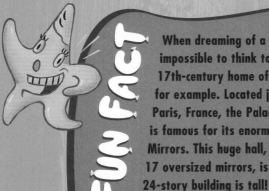

Dear _____,

_____! My new dream
①
②
house is finally finished and I'm all moved
in—it took only _____ years to build.
③
You're always welcome to visit me here in

_____. The house is easy to find—just
④
look for the _____
⑤
outside. Oh, and don't
be frightened by the _____
⑥
in the front
yard—its name is _____
⑦
and it wouldn't hurt
a fly! Take a snooze under the _____,
⑧
and stop to smell a(n) _____
⑨
or two. (I planted them myself.) Bring as many
people as you'd like. With _____
⑩
bedrooms, there's plenty of room for everyone!
My new address is _____
⑪

_____ Street,
⑫
_____-ville, Earth.
your name
I hope to see you soon!

_____
your signature

FIND A FRIEND!

ASK YOUR FRIEND FOR ANSWERS TO
THE FILL-IN-THE-BLANKS STORY, THEN
READ THE STORY ALOUD!

Master Plan for _____ JoeY _____ 's Dream House _____
　　　　　　　　　　　　your name　　　　　　　　　　today's date

Write it!

For each blank, roll one of the letter cubes, then fill in the blank with a word that starts with the letter you rolled.

My new house is located in _____. It's so big that
　　　　　　　　　　　　　　country

it has a full-size _____ inside—I'll never miss out
　　　　　　　　　restaurant

on _____ again! There's also a theater, so I
　　　food

can watch _____ any time I want. And outside
　　　　　movie

there's a huge _____—shaped fountain!
　　　　　　　　　animal

Draw it!

Your dream house is all yours, and you get to make it whatever you want it to be. Answer the questions below to give more detail to your dream house, then use the drawing space to draw your new pad.

- Where would you like to live?

• By the beach?

• In the mountains?

• In the jungle?

• In a tree?

• Underwater?

- How would you make your house instantly recognizable to anyone walking by?

- What kinds of trees and flowers would be in your garden?

- Would you like a pool?

- What kinds of animals would live in your yard?

How Now, House?

How do you feel about the real place where you live? Do some research to check out what you like best, what's unique, and what you'd like to change.

I live in a(n) _____.

It has _____ bathrooms, _____ bedrooms, and a(n) _____.

It also has a(n) _____.

My favorite thing about where I live is

_____.

My home is the only one I know of with a(n) _____.

If I could change one thing about where I live, I would

_____
_____
_____
_____.

Solve it!

Find all of the things that might be in your dream backyard.

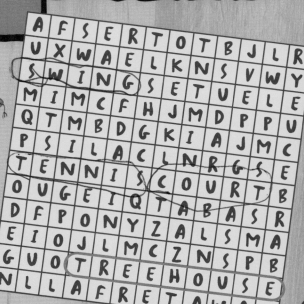

Turn to page 36 to check your answers.

WEATHER WATCHER

Neither snow nor rain nor heat will keep you from pulling together this amazing weather report!

There's nothing quite so refreshing as a dip in a mud puddle after a good hard rain!

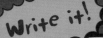

Write it!

Weather reporters use lots of different words to describe the weather. There's the temperature, the color of the sky, the type of clouds, whether it is rainy, sunny, or snowing—the list could go on and on. Answer the following questions to create your own weather report on the opposite page!

1. An unusual pet
2. A word describing what it looks like under your bed
3. A word describing your socks
4. Something that makes a lot of noise
5. A word describing how you feel right now
6. Something that happens only once in a while

7. Something you might find in a backyard
8. Your shoe size
9. An animal whose name begins with a letter on one of the letter cubes
10. A word describing someone in your family
11. A word describing your hair
12. Your least favorite kind of weather

FIND A FRIEND!

ASK A FRIEND TO ANSWER THESE QUESTIONS—BUT KEEP THE PAGE HIDDEN. THEN READ BACK YOUR FRIEND'S CUSTOMIZED WEATHER REPORT IN YOUR BEST TV VOICE! MIX IT UP—TRY READING WITH AN ACCENT, OR IN A WHISPER, OR IN THE HIGHEST OR LOWEST VOICE YOU CAN MUSTER!

AND NOW, THE WEATHER!

Good evening, ladies and _____. This is
1

_____ with a look at our weather! Today
your name

was _____ and _____,
2   3

with _____ reported in the
4

outlying areas. Tonight we can expect partly

_____ skies with a chance of
5

_____ around midnight. Get ready for
6

a full moon tonight—and bring in those plants and

_____, as the temperatures may get
7

as low as _____. More of the same
8

tomorrow until a front rolls in and we can expect it

to rain cats and _____. We're looking
9

at a(n) _____ weekend with
10

_____ skies and little chance of
11

_____. And that's our weather!
12

Back to the rest of today's activities.

RW
21

Record it!

Record today's weather data: _____ _____
date   time

Describe the weather conditions:

Color in the thermometer to show today's temperature

Is it rainy?   Sunny?   Cloudy?   Windy?

_____

_____

_____

Clothing item most needed today:

☐ shorts   ☐ swimsuit

☐ sweater   ☐ raincoat

☐ parka

Thermometer: 100 90 80 70 60 50 40 30 20 10 0

Draw it! Imagine you are setting off on a journey around the world—and beyond. How do you know what to pack? By predicting the weather, of course! Pick the places you'll visit, then draw what the weather will be like there.

_____'S EXTENDED TRAVEL FORECAST
your name

_____ someplace where it's always warm	_____ someplace where it's always cold	_____ someplace you've never been to but have always wanted to visit
Three pieces of clothing you'll need:	Three pieces of clothing you'll need:	Three pieces of clothing you'll need:
1. _____	1. _____	1. _____
2. _____	2. _____	2. _____
3. _____	3. _____	3. _____

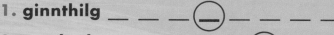

SCRAMBLED WEATHER

Can you unscramble the
weather words below?

FIND A FRIEND!

1. **ginnthilg** _ _ _ _ _(_)_ _ _
2. **runthed** _ _ _ _ _ _(_)_
3. **scludo** _ _ _ _ _(_)_
4. **dwin** _(_)_ _ _
5. **ahli** _ _ _ _
6. **swon** _ _ _(_)_
7. **gof** _ _ _
8. **niar** _(_)_ _ _
9. **hisesunn** _ _(_)_ _ _ _ _ _

Now unscramble the circled letters to reveal a
weather word for which April is commonly known!

_ _ _ _ _ _ _ _ _

❓ Turn to page 36 to check your answers.

IT'S A TWISTER!
TAKE TURNS DOING THIS
TONGUE-TWISTER WITH A
FRIEND. TRY SAYING IT
THREE TIMES QUICKLY
WITHOUT MESSING UP
ANY WORDS: "WHETHER
THE WEATHER IS COOL,
OR WHETHER THE
WEATHER IS HOT,
WE'LL BE TOGETHER,
WHATEVER THE WEATHER,
WHETHER WE LIKE IT OR
NOT!" WHO CAN SAY IT
THE FASTEST? WHO CAN
SAY IT THE MOST TIMES
IN A ROW WITHOUT
MESSING UP?

FUN FACT

You may have heard of the expression
"raining cats and dogs," but how about
raining frogs? It isn't just a saying—it
really happens! Such a phenomenon has
been reported in Mexico, England, and
France. Scientists think tornadoes yank the
frogs from their ponds and lakes up into the
clouds, then drop them back to the ground.

Photo: Corbis

AT THE MOVIES

Write it!

Ready...action! The camera is rolling and there's a movie that needs a close-up on your witty wordplay.

Word Worm started writing this movie review but had to wriggle on out to judge a spelling bee. Answer the questions below and plug them into the review!

1. A word describing your lunch

2. Something you like to do that ends in -ing

3. A place you really love to go

4. The first name of your favorite actor

5. A chore you don't like doing

6. The name of the town or city where you live

7. What you would like to be when you grow up

8. The age of the youngest person in your family

9. Someone you know who is really funny

10. Something you like to ride in

11. Something in your room that needs to be thrown out

12. A movie you like but don't love

13. A food you could eat every day without getting sick of

14. An animal you would find in a barn

15. What you say when you get something you really want

16. A sound that the animal from #14 makes

17. A part of your body where there is a freckle or a mole

18. The name of one of your favorite relatives

19. A planet other than Earth

Try answering a few different ways—new answers will give you a whole new review!

FIND A FRIEND!

WRITE DOWN YOUR THREE FAVORITE MOVIES, THEN WRITE DOWN WHAT YOU THINK YOUR FRIEND'S THREE FAVORITE MOVIES ARE. HAVE YOUR FRIEND DO THE SAME THING. COMPARE YOUR ANSWERS—HOW WELL DO YOU KNOW EACH OTHER'S TASTE IN MOVIES?

I just saw "The _____ Journey," and let me tell you—if
                          1

you're looking for a movie that makes you feel like _____, this is
                                                                    2

the one for you. You'll laugh, you'll cry, you'll even forget all about your upcoming trip to

_____.
          3

The drama begins when a man named _____ decides to give up his current job
                                                          4

_____ and move to _____ to try to
          5   6

make it as a(n) _____. After _____ months, things start looking up
                          7   8

when he gets a job babysitting for _____. The hilarity starts when the two of them decide to build a
                                                9

_____ out of _____ and, amazingly, the thing works!
          10   11

This movie is better than watching _____ but not as good as eating _____
                                                12   13

all day on a tropical beach. My advice: Bring the parents, bring the grandparents, bring the _____.
                                                                                                          14

They'll all say "_____" or "_____" and thank you for recommending this
                        15   16

_____-warming film. I can't wait for the sequel: "_____ on
          17   18

_____"!
          19

I give it _____ out of 3 fezzes.
                roll the die

THIS IS MY
FAVORITE PART!

RW

25

NOW PLAYING!

Star Cinema

Starring _____, _____,
your name   your best friend's name

and _____.
your favorite movie star

"Wiggle on down to your nearest theater and see this movie!" — *Word Worm Bugle*

RW

26

Draw it!

Create your own movie poster in the drawing frame. Start by drawing a poster for the movie you helped Word Worm review. Don't forget to add the title and names of the stars. Once you've warmed up a bit, come up with a poster for your own movie. Use some of these ideas to get you started:

- Put yourself and your friends in a movie. You can make the movie about something that really happened, but change the setting to something really wacky—like another planet.

- Think of two movies you love, and try combining them into one movie.

- Think of something really funny that happened to you this week, and turn it into an idea for a movie.

FIND A FRIEND!

Have your friend fill in the top of the poster, and you get to draw the picture. Then draw the picture first and have your friend come up with a title. Now switch. Your movie will be a true meeting of the minds!

Most of the sounds you hear in a movie, from footsteps to rain, are added after a scene is filmed. A sound effects expert called a Foley artist finds ingenious ways to recreate the sounds from a movie right in the studio. Can you match each sound to how it can be made?

Solve it!

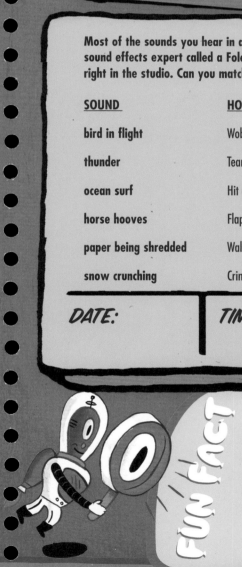

SOUND	HOW IT IS MADE
bird in flight	Wobble a cookie sheet.
thunder	Tear cabbage.
ocean surf	Hit empty coconut shells against a flat surface.
horse hooves	Flap together a pair of leather gloves.
paper being shredded	Walk on cornstarch in a burlap bag.
snow crunching	Crinkle a thin plastic bag.

DATE: *TIME:*   *TAKE:*

 Turn to page 36 to check your answers.

FUN FACT

Movie snacks come in many varieties around the world. In Thailand theatergoers chew on dried squid strips, in Australia they munch on meat pies, and in much of Europe they eat popcorn with sugar on it instead of salt.

Photo: Corbis

ROAD TRIP

What's the best road trip you can imagine? It's time to hit the open road and see how your latest adventure takes shape!

A postcard is worth a thousand words. I'll find a way to make them all fit!

Write it!

One of the best things about a road trip is writing postcards to your friends! You can describe all the things you see, eat, and do on your journeys—or tell funny stories your friends won't believe happened. Help Word Worm finish this letter by writing your answers in the blanks on the next page.

1. A cool feature you'd want in your fantasy car
2. Your favorite drink
3. Something you never travel without
4. Your favorite snack
5. A place you've always wanted to visit but never have
6. A book or movie character you'd love to meet
7. A food that starts with a letter you roll using one of your letter cubes
8. Something you wish you had in your room
9. A planet in outer space
10. The number of minutes it takes you to decide what to order in a restaurant
11. Something you can find in a bathroom
12. Something you're always glad to come home to

Sculpt it!

Use the Cranium Clay to make a sculpture of a car you'd love to travel in.

FUN FACT

The World's Largest Buffalo, a cement sculpture that weighs more than 60 tons, stands by the highway in Jamestown, North Dakota. There must be something in the water in North Dakota: You can also see a giant cow, giant pheasants, a giant crane, and a giant grasshopper there!

Dear Star Performer, Creative Cat, and Data Head,

You won't believe what an awesome time we're having on this trip. First of all, we're traveling in a car full of unusual features like _____, and it's
1
powered by _____, which of
2
course we always have plenty of! We've brought along everything we need to have a good time, including my _____ and tons
3
of _____ to snack on.
4

My whole life I've always wanted to go to _____, so is it any surprise
5
that we went there first? It was even more incredible than I imagined. And to top it all off, _____ was there and invited us
6
over for _____. What a treat!
7

That night, we stayed in a motel where every room had _____. My dream come true!
8

The next day, we stopped at an amusement park called Art Park. There was a ride there unlike any one I'd ever been on. It looked like a futuristic rocket, and it took us straight to _____ in only
9
_____ seconds! After that, we drove over to
10
the nearby Museum of _____.
11
The place was a little strange, but definitely interesting!

We're headed home soon. I don't really want this trip to end, but it will be nice to get back because I do miss my _____—and all of you too!
12

Sincerely,

Word Worm

LOOK!

DON'T MISS **THIS** ROADSIDE WONDER!

YOU'RE SO CLOSE—

JUST TAKE THE NEXT EXIT!

WORLD'S LARGEST

JUST AHEAD!

RW

Draw it! What attractions would you visit on your perfect road trip? Or on the world's funniest road trip? Here's your chance to dream them up. Draw pictures of your new roadside attractions on the billboards, and add some words to make people want to stop. Use these ideas to get you started:

- Invent a new kind of road food or theme restaurant.
- Come up with a fun motel—is it in a special shape, or does it have special entertainment?
- Make up something that could be the World's Largest.
- Think of a roadside attraction just for pets.
- Create a wacky museum that never existed before.

WHAT OTHER GREAT ROADSIDE ATTRACTIONS WOULD YOU STOP THE CAR FOR? USE YOUR IMAGINATION TO CREATE THEM!

Solve it! Match these U.S. highway signs to their definitions.

1. _____
2. _____
3. _____

4. _____
5. _____
6. _____

A. Slippery When Wet

B. Playground

C. Camping

D. Roadside Table

E. Deer Crossing

F. Trail

Turn to page 36 to check your answers.

Play it! Wonder what you would take on the ultimate road trip? Make a list by rolling one letter cube at a time and coming up with things that start with each letter you rolled.

FIND A FRIEND! TRY PLAYING THIS PACKING LIST GAME WITH A FRIEND: THINK OF ITEMS YOU'D TAKE ON YOUR TRIP, AND SAY ONE THAT BEGINS WITH THE LETTER A. CONTINUE YOUR LIST—EACH ADDITIONAL ITEM BEGINS WITH THE NEXT LETTER IN THE ALPHABET. IF YOU GET STUCK, YOUR FRIEND GETS TO START WHERE YOU LEFT OFF. WHO CAN GET TO Z FIRST?

Word Worm's Super Sign-In Pages

Now that you've had a chance to play around with words, it's time for your friends and family members to do the same with **WORD WORM'S SUPER SIGN-IN PAGES**. The questions are quick and fun to fill out—see how many people you can get to sign in, and don't forget to write in your own answers!

Sign in! Answer the questions below and write your name, along with a unique artistic symbol that you'll use to identify yourself throughout **WORD WORM'S SUPER SIGN-IN PAGES**. On each page that follows, draw your symbol after your answer!

If you could take only one book to a desert island, what would you choose?

What foreign language would you like to learn?

If you were to write the story of your life, what would the first sentence be?

What's your favorite place to read?

Write down your favorite rhyme or poem.

What pen name would you choose if you wrote a book?

If you could write a book about any of your friends or family, whom would you write about, and why?

What else do you want to know about your friends and family?

_____

Write your own question here!

? Answer Page

You've found the answer page! Once you've finished an activity, check your answers here.

Out of This World: Planetary Pop Quiz (page 11)

1. **False.** Saturn is not the only planet with rings: Jupiter, Uranus, and Neptune have rings too! Galileo, the first person to see Saturn's rings, thought they were attached to the planet rather than floating around it. He described them as "handles."

2. **True.** The Sun is really a star! Even though it is gigantic compared to Earth, it is average-sized for a star. It just looks so enormous in the sky compared to other stars because it is the closest one to Earth.

3. **False.** The Moon and Earth are about the same age: 4.6 billion years old. You'd need a pretty big cake to hold all those birthday candles!

Out of This World: Solve it! (page 11)

Mercury, Venus, Earth, Mars, Jupiter, Saturn, Uranus, Neptune, Pluto

Silly Superheroes: A-Mazing Superhero (page 15)

START

FINISH

Weather Watcher: Scrambled Weather (page 23)

1. lightning
2. thunder
3. clouds
4. wind
5. hail
6. snow
7. fog
8. rain
9. sunshine

April is known for **showers**!

At the Movies: Solve it! (page 27)

BIRD IN FLIGHT	WOBBLE A COOKIE SHEET.
THUNDER	TEAR CABBAGE.
OCEAN SURF	HIT EMPTY COCONUT SHELLS AGAINST A FLAT SURFACE.
HORSE HOOVES	FLAP TOGETHER A PAIR OF LEATHER GLOVES.
PAPER BEING SHREDDED	WALK ON CORNSTARCH IN A BURLAP BAG.
SNOW CRUNCHING	CRINKLE A THIN PLASTIC BAG.

Road Trip: Solve it! (page 31)

1-C, 2-E, 3-B, 4-D, 5-A, 6-F

Dream House: Solve it! (page 19)

A	F	S	E	R	T	O	T	B	J	L	R
U	X	W	A	E	L	K	N	S	V	W	Y
S	W	I	N	G	S	E	T	U	E	L	E
M	I	M	C	F	H	J	M	D	P	P	U
Q	T	M	B	D	G	K	I	A	J	M	C
P	S	I	L	A	C	L	N	R	G	S	E
T	E	N	N	I	S	C	O	U	R	T	B
O	U	G	E	I	Q	T	A	B	A	S	R
D	F	P	O	N	Y	Z	A	L	S	M	A
E	I	O	J	L	M	C	Z	N	S	P	B
G	U	O	T	R	E	E	H	O	U	S	E
N	L	L	A	F	R	E	T	A	W	A	C

barbecue
grass
pony
slide
swimming pool
swing set
tennis court
tree house
waterfall

Welcome to Cranium Mini Letter Line-Up!
Grab your friends, slide out the game board,
and have some outrageous fun!

OBJECT OF THE GAME

Get your team to
cross the **FINISH** line.

GET READY

① Slide out the game board from the back cover. Make sure that the clear plastic game sheet is attached.

② Set out the mover piece, timer, die, game cards, and letter cubes. You will need a pen or pencil and a sheet of paper.

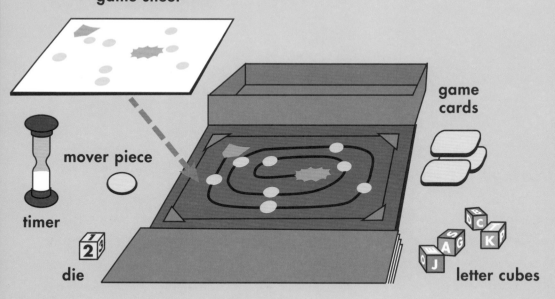

game sheet

mover piece

timer

die

game cards

letter cubes

③ Place the mover piece on the **START** space, and place the cards face down in a draw pile.

④ The player whose birthday is coming up next goes first.

ON YOUR TURN

In Mini Letter Line-Up, everyone plays together as one team.

① **Draw a card.** Read the activity instructions on the card out loud.

② When you're ready, **start the timer.** You'll write down your team's answers.

③ **If your team successfully completes the activity before time runs out,** roll the die and **move forward** the number of spaces you rolled. Your turn is over, and the player to your left goes next. **If your team does not successfully complete the activity before time runs out,** your turn is over, and the player to your left goes next.

④ Put the card you just played in a discard pile.

HOW TO WIN

When you cross the **FINISH** line, congratulations—you've won Mini Letter Line-Up!

SPECIAL MEGA-COMBO GAME!

If you or a friend have the **Creative Cat, Data Head, or Star Performer Books of Outrageous Fun!,** you can combine them to make one outrageously fun game! Simply lay one or more of the game sheets from the other books on top of this one to make a single game board. Place the cards from each game face down in their own draw piles.

Roll the die and move to start the game. In this version, you'll do the activity that matches the color of the space you're on. Then follow the regular rules to play this mega-combo game!

TRY IT!
If you have at least four players you can try playing as two teams! Each team selects a mover piece and places it on the START space. The first team to cross the FINISH line wins the game! The rest of the rules stay the same.